ARGENTINA

By Theia Lake and
Joanne Mattern

EXPLORING WORLD CULTURES

Cavendish Square

Published in 2025 by Cavendish Square Publishing, LLC
2544 Clinton Street, Buffalo, NY 14224

Second Edition

Website: cavendishsq.com

Library of Congress Cataloging-in-Publication Data

Names: Lake, Theia, author. | Mattern, Joanne, 1963- author.
Title: Argentina / Theia Lake, Joanne Mattern.
Description: Second edition. | [Buffalo, New York] : Cavendish Square Publishing, [2025] | Series: Exploring world cultures | Includes bibliographical references and index.
Identifiers: LCCN 2024008685 (print) | LCCN 2024008686 (ebook) | ISBN 9781502670984 (library binding) | ISBN 9781502670977 (paperback) | ISBN 9781502670991 (ebook)
Subjects: LCSH: Argentina--Juvenile literature.
Classification: LCC F2808.2 .M38 2025 (print) | LCC F2808.2 (ebook) | DDC 982--dc23/eng/20240326
LC record available at https://lccn.loc.gov/2024008685
LC ebook record available at https://lccn.loc.gov/2024008686

Writers: Joanne Mattern; Theia Lake (second edition)
Editor: Theresa Emminizer
Copyeditor: Danielle Haynes
Designer: Andrea Davison-Bartolotta

The photographs in this book are used by permission and through the courtesy of: Cover LeoPatrizi/iStockphoto.com; p. 4 Dudarev Mikhail/Shutterstock.com; p. 5 Spectral-Design/Shutterstock.com; p. 6 Jonak/Shutterstock.com; p. 7 Tupungato/Shutterstock.com; p. 8 Ricardo_Dias/Shutterstock.com; p. 9 Maia Ocampo/Shutterstock.com; p. 10 saiko3p/Shutterstock.com; p. 11 Martina Abrego/Shutterstock.com; p. 12 Andrzej Rostek/Shutterstock.com; p. 13 Alexandr Vorobev/Shutterstock.com; p. 15 (top), 27 sunsinger/Shutterstock.com; p. 15 (bottom) R.M. Nunes/Shutterstock.com; p. 16 Gonzalo Bell/Shutterstock.com; p. 17 LiAndStudio/Shutterstock.com; p. 18 T photography/Shutterstock.com; p. 19 Sobrevolando Patagonia/Shutterstock.com; p. 20 Sandra Moraes/Shutterstock.com; p. 21 Mark Green/Shutterstock.com; p. 22 art of line/Shutterstock.com; p. 23 Autumn Sky Photography/Shutterstock.com; p. 24 Ale Grutta foto/Shutterstock.com; p. 25 Kobby Dagan/Shutterstock.com; p. 26 UladzimirZuyeu/Shutterstock.com; p. 28 AlexCorv/Shutterstock.com; p. 29 Marcus Z-pics/Shutterstock.com.

CPSIA compliance information: Batch #CS25CSQ: For further information contact Cavendish Square Publishing LLC at 1-877-980-4450.

Printed in the United States of America

CONTENTS

INTRODUCTION

Argentina is a beautiful country located in the southern part of South America. Found between the Andes Mountains and the Atlantic Ocean, its wide-ranging lands feature waterfalls and lakes, mountains and plains, and even glaciers!

The word Argentina means "silvery." Spanish **explorers** chose the name because they thought there was a lot of silver in the land.

Argentina is known for its breathtaking scenery, or sights.

Today, Argentina is home to about 46 million people. People who live in Argentina are called Argentines. Many Argentines are immigrants, or people who moved there from other countries. Though Spanish is the country's official language, people speak other languages there as well.

Argentine **culture** has been shaped by the country's **geography**, history, and people. Its tasty food, beautiful music, and moving art are just a few of the things that make Argentina so special. Argentine dance, sports, and celebrations draw visitors from across the world to this one-of-a-kind country.

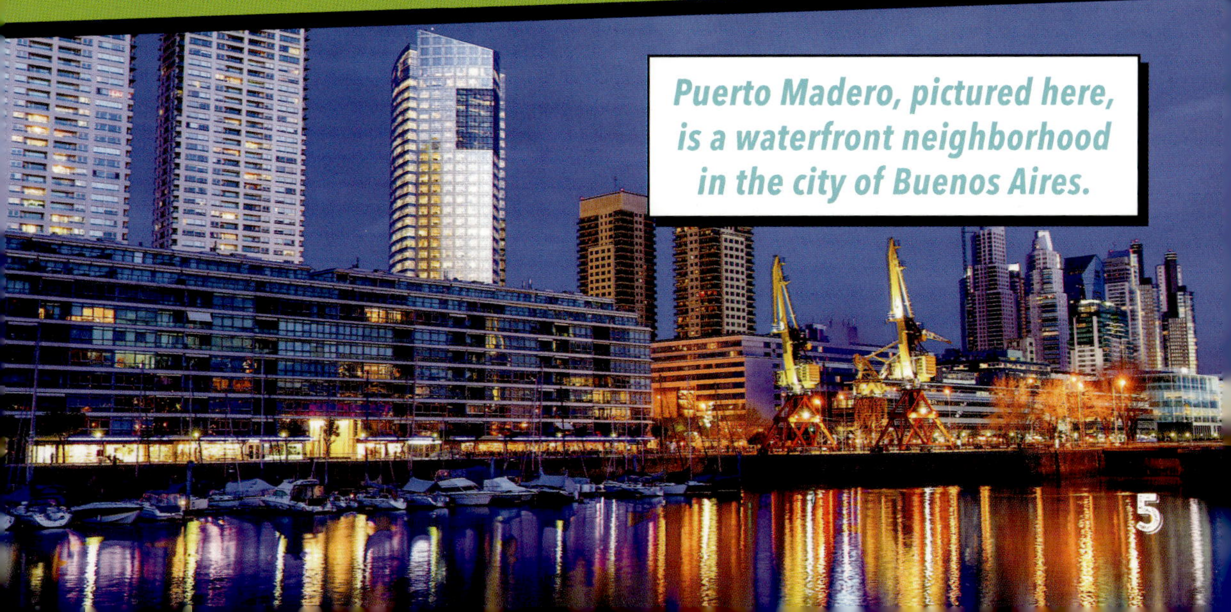

Puerto Madero, pictured here, is a waterfront neighborhood in the city of Buenos Aires.

GEOGRAPHY

Argentina is shaped a bit like an upside-down triangle. It covers 1,073,518 square miles (2,780,400 square kilometers). Argentina's geography can be grouped into main areas: the Andes, the Chaco, Mesopotamia, the Pampas, and Patagonia.

FACT!

The Strait of Magellan separates a small group of islands called Tierra del Fuego from the rest of Argentina.

Aconcagua is the highest mountain in Argentina. It's 22,831 feet (6,959 meters) tall.

The Andes Mountains run along the border between Argentina and Chile. The Chaco is a hot, dry plain. Mesopotamia is a **lowland** between the Paraná and the Uruguay Rivers. The Pampas are flat grasslands across the middle of the country. Patagonia is a cold, windy area.

Argentina is surrounded by Uruguay, Brazil, Paraguay, Bolivia, and Chile.

PATAGONIA

Travelers from all over the world come to Patagonia to see its beautiful glaciers. The Andes **ice cap** is the third-largest glacier field in the world. Los Glaciares National Park is the largest national park in Argentina. The Perito Moreno Glacier is found there.

HISTORY

Indigenous, or native, peoples lived in Argentina long before the Spanish explorers arrived during the 1500s. Some were nomadic, meaning they moved from place to place. Others were farmers.

Ferdinand Magellan was one of the first Europeans to explore Argentina. In 1536, explorer Pedro de Mendoza led 2,000 settlers to Argentina. They founded the city of Buenos Aires.

FACT!

Far-right leader Javier Milei became president of Argentina in December 2023. He claims he'll make big changes to the country.

The Cave of the Hands in Patagonia, Argentina, shows cave paintings dating back 13,000 years.

Argentina's president lives in the Casa Rosada in Buenos Aires.

Spain ruled Argentina until 1816. After Argentina became independent, different groups fought for power. For many years, the military ran the government. Today, it's led by a president.

PERONISM

Peronism is an Argentine political movement based on the ideas of former president Juan Perón. Perón became president in 1946. He and his wife, Eva Perón, became very popular. Though military leaders overthrew Perón in 1955, the Peronist movement and party still have strong support in Argentina.

GOVERNMENT

Buenos Aires is the capital of Argentina. Argentina is a union of 23 provinces, or territories. Each province has a local government. The federal, or national, government makes most of the country's laws.

Argentina's federal government has three parts: executive, legislative, and judicial. The executive branch carries out laws. The president is the head of this branch. The people of Argentina elect the president and vice president.

The Palace of the Argentine National Congress (Palacio del Congreso) is pictured here. This is where members of the legislative branch meet.

The legislative branch makes laws. It has two parts, called houses. Argentines also elect members of these houses.

The judicial branch decides legal matters.

FACT!

Similar to the federal government, each provincial government is made up of executive, legislative, and judicial branches.

The Argentine flag was updated slightly in 2010, when the blue stripes were darkened, and the sun picture was redesigned.

THE ARGENTINE CONSTITUTION

Argentina's leaders created the country's first **constitution** in 1853. They modeled it after the U.S. Constitution. The Argentine Constitution has been changed since then, including a 1994 change allowing for **consecutive** presidential terms.

THE ECONOMY

Argentina's economy is based on factories, farming, **ranching**, and tourism, or travel.

Argentine beef is sold all over the world. Farmers also grow wheat, lemons, peanuts, grapes, and many other crops.

FACT!

Brazil is Argentina's most important partner in trade. Other big trade partners include China, the United States, Chile, and Germany.

Argentine paper money is called the peso. Coins are called centavos.

INFLATION

Inflation means that the price of things is rising. That means people need to pay more money for goods and services than they used to. The current inflation rate in Argentina is 211 percent. Argentine pesos are being devalued, meaning they aren't worth as much. One Argentine peso is equal to 0.12 U.S. cent.

Many Argentines work in factories. Workers make cars, car parts, steel, plastic goods, and leather. Argentina's mines produce lead, zinc, iron ore, gold, and copper. Patagonia produces a large amount of oil.

Over the years, the Argentine economy has had several downturns. Recently, inflation has been a major problem. As prices rise, more people are put at risk, or in danger, of **poverty**.

This is the Ministry (office) of Economy building in Buenos Aires.

THE ENVIRONMENT

Argentina's **environment** is made up of high mountains, rainforests, flat plains, and volcanic hills. The plants and animals that live there are as varied as the land.

Argentina is home to large cats such as jaguars, howler monkeys, and more! Crocodiles and flamingos live in some rivers and lakes. Seals and orca whales live near the glaciers in the south.

More than 1,000 kinds of birds live in Argentina. Parrots and toucans live in the rainforest. Penguins live on islands off the coast. Many birds live in national parks.

NATIONAL PARKS

There are 36 national parks in Argentina. The wildlife and land in these areas are protected, or kept safe, by law. Visitors to Argentina's national parks can enjoy hiking, biking, swimming, and watching wildlife. Parque Nacional Nahuel Huapi is Argentina's oldest national park. It was founded, or made, in 1934.

Parque Nacional (National Park) Iberá is a safe place for wildlife, such as the caiman and capybara pictured here.

FACT!

Patagonian cypress trees, also called alerce, are some of the oldest and biggest trees in the world. They can live more than 3,000 years!

The waterfalls at Parque Nacional Iguazú are surrounded by rainforest, but visitors can walk close to the beautiful falls on boardwalks.

THE PEOPLE TODAY

Who are the Argentine people? They come from a few different **ethnic** backgrounds. Most Argentines are descended, or come from, European immigrants, mainly from Spain and Italy. Others came from surrounding countries, such as Paraguay, Bolivia, and Chile.

FACT!

In recent years, Argentina's population growth has slowed down. The country's birth rate is falling, meaning that fewer babies are being born.

This picture shows a little girl at school in the Chaco Province of Argentina.

Many Argentines are Mestizo. Mestizo is a word used to describe people with both European and Native backgrounds. Native people (sometimes called Amerindians) make up a small part of the population. An even smaller number of people are of African descent.

NATIVE PEOPLE

There are about 35 different Indigenous groups in Argentina. The Mapuche, Quechua, Guaraní, Wichí, and Toba people are a few. Each group has its own language and **traditions**. Indigenous communities have faced many hardships including displacement (being forcibly removed from traditional lands) and discrimination (unfair treatment).

Argentine soccer fans celebrate in the streets of Buenos Aires.

LIFESTYLE

Most people in Argentina live in cities. About one-third of Argentina's population lives in or near Buenos Aires. Buenos Aires feels a lot like a city in Europe. There are tall, modern buildings. Stores and restaurants line the roads. Cars and buses fill the busy streets.

FACT!

Argentine cowboys are called gauchos. Gauchos work hard in tough conditions. The gaucho is an important part of Argentine culture.

Colorful houses line Caminito Street in La Boca, a neighborhood of Buenos Aires.

About one-third of Argentines live along the rivers in the north. Another third live in the south and west. Most of these areas are used for farming or ranching. Very few people live in Patagonia.

EDUCATION

Argentine children go to school from March to November. They have summer vacation in December, January, and February. Children have to go to school between the ages of 6 and 14. Students study math, science, Spanish, and history. They also learn to speak, read, and write in English.

A gaucho works with a herd of cows in Patagonia.

RELIGION

The Roman Catholic religion, or belief system, is a big part of Argentine culture. Argentines celebrate Catholic holidays, such as Christmas and Easter. Many towns have **patron saints**. People honor these saints with parades. They also visit holy places to say special prayers.

FACT!
The Miracle Festival is a Catholic event in Salta. It celebrates Mary, the mother of Jesus.

The Metropolitan Cathedral is the main Catholic church in Buenos Aires.

Other religious groups include Protestants, Jews, and Muslims. The number of Protestants has been growing since the 1960s. Mormons are another large Christian group in the country. Although only about 5 percent of the population is Jewish, Argentina has the largest Jewish community in South America.

In May 2013, a billboard in Buenos Aires celebrates Pope Francis being named pope.

POPE FRANCIS

Pope Francis is the leader of the Roman Catholic Church. He became pope in 2013. Pope Francis was born Jorge Mario Bergoglio on December 17, 1936, in Buenos Aires. His parents were Italian immigrants to Argentina. Pope Francis is the first pope from South America.

LANGUAGE

Spanish is the main language spoken in Argentina. However, like in other Latin American countries, Argentine Spanish has its own unique words and accent, or way of speaking. This is known as a language dialect. The Argentine Spanish dialect is sometimes called Rioplatense Spanish. That's because it comes from the Rio de la Plata area between Argentina and Uruguay.

FACT!
There are at least 14 Indigenous languages spoken in Argentina. Quechua is likely the most widely spoken Indigenous language.

This sign on the border between Argentina and Chile says "Welcome to the Republic of Argentina" in Spanish.

The visitor center at Puerto Iguazú shows the park's Guaraní name, Yvyra Reta, meaning "land of trees."

Many people in Argentina also speak other languages. These languages include Italian, German, and French. English is also widely spoken in Argentina. Indigenous languages are spoken as well.

INDIGENOUS LANGUAGES

Traditional Indigenous languages are still spoken in Argentina today. People in the northwest areas of Argentina may speak Quechua. This language was spoken by the ancient Inca Empire in Peru. Guaraní is spoken in the northeastern provinces. Mapudungun is the language of the Mapuche people in southern Argentina.

ARTS AND FESTIVALS

If you want to experience Argentine culture, go to the **Folklore** National Festival in Cosquín! The celebration is kicked off by a big parade and lasts several days. People wear beautiful, traditional costumes and eat traditional food. In addition, musicians play traditional music!

FACT!

Carnaval is a Catholic festival observed in many South American countries. It's also popular in Argentina. People celebrate by going to parades, dressing colorfully, and dancing to live music.

These sculptures in the center of Cosquín show popular singers Mercedes Sosa and Jorge Cafrune.

In September 2023, the 20th Mundial de Tango, or Tango World Cup, was held in Buenos Aires.

Argentine folk music includes many different styles such as zamba, chacarera, and gato. People come to this festival from far and near to dance, sing, and celebrate Argentina's rich and beautiful folklore traditions.

THE TANGO FESTIVAL

The Tango Festival is held in Buenos Aires every year in August. During this exciting event, the best dancers come from all over the world to show off their moves across the city. Visitors can take dance classes, watch shows, and learn about the history of tango.

FUN AND PLAY

Polo, basketball, and football, or soccer, are all popular sports in Argentina. Argentines Lionel Messi and Diego Maradona are considered some of the greatest soccer players of all time. They both won World Cups for Argentina.

PATO

The name *pato* means duck in Spanish. The game of pato, which is very popular in Argentina, used to be played with a duck instead of a ball! Today, the ball is made of leather. The game was made up by gauchos in the 1700s.

Football fans in Buenos Aires celebrate winning the FIFA World Cup in 2022.

Argentina's national sport is called *pato*. Pato players ride horses. While they ride, they try to throw a ball into the other team's goal.

Tennis, field hockey, and rugby are also popular sports. Argentina's beautiful beaches and mountains make it a popular place to go swimming and skiing as well.

FACT!
The modern game of pato was introduced during the 1930s. Today's game is safer and has more rules.

These men are playing pato during a festival in Buenos Aires.

FOOD

Argentine food often features tasty beef from Argentine cattle ranches. Asado is a traditional dish. It's a way of barbecuing, or grilling, meat that takes several hours.

SWEET TREATS

Argentines also like sweets. They often top cakes with a sweet caramel called *dulce de leche*. Dulce de leche means "candy made from milk." Alfajor is another favorite sweet treat. An alfajor is a cookie sandwich with chocolate in the middle that is then dipped in melted chocolate.

"Asado" is both a way of grilling meat and the word used to describe gathering around the barbecue with friends.

Carbonada is a stew made of meat, potatoes, sweet potatoes, and corn on the cob. Empanadas, or meat pies, are also popular. People often bring empanadas on picnics. It's tasty to dip empanadas in chimichurri, which is a sauce made of oil, **vinegar**, parsley, and spices.

Dinner is served late in Argentina—usually around 9:00 or 10:00 at night!

FACT!

Yerba mate is a popular drink in Argentina. It's a tea made from leaves and twigs of the mate plant.

*Mate is often sipped through a metal straw in a cup made from a **gourd**.*

GLOSSARY

consecutive: Happening in a row or one after another.

constitution: The basic laws by which a country, state, or group is governed.

culture: The beliefs and ways of life of a certain group of people.

environment: The natural world around us.

ethnic: Of or relating to large groups of people who have the same cultural background and ways of life.

explorer: Someone who searches something to find out more about a place.

folklore: Ideas or stories that may not be true but that many people have heard or read.

geography: The land and its features.

gourd: A fruit with a hard rind.

ice cap: A cover of permanent ice and snow.

lowland: Low or level (flat) country.

patron saint: A religious figure who protects a person or a place.

poverty: The state of being poor.

ranching: A type of farming in which cattle, sheep, horses, or other livestock are raised on open land.

tradition: A way of thinking, behaving, or doing something that's been used by people in a particular society for a long time.

vinegar: A sour liquid made by fermentation.

FIND OUT MORE

Books

Godward, Mary, and Robert Hamwee. *Argentina: The Essential Guide to Customs and Culture*. London, UK: Kuperard, 2023.

Kelin, Allan. *Fodor's Essential Argentina: With the Wine Country, Uruguay & Chilean Patagonia*. New York, NY: Fodor's Travel, 2023.

Websites

Britannica: Argentina
www.britannica.com/place/Argentina
Learn more about Argentina's history.

Lonely Planet: Argentina
www.lonelyplanet.com/argentina
Learn more about all there is to see and do in Argentina.

Video

Argentine Tango Championship
tangousachampionship.com/photo-videos/
Watch dancers from the 2021 Tango Festival!

Publisher's note to educators and parents: Our editors have carefully reviewed these websites to ensure that they are suitable for students. Many websites change frequently, however, and we cannot guarantee that a site's future contents will continue to meet our high standards of quality and educational value. Be advised that students should be closely supervised whenever they access the internet.

INDEX